INVENTIONS
in science

  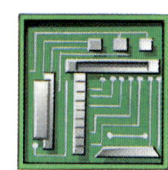  

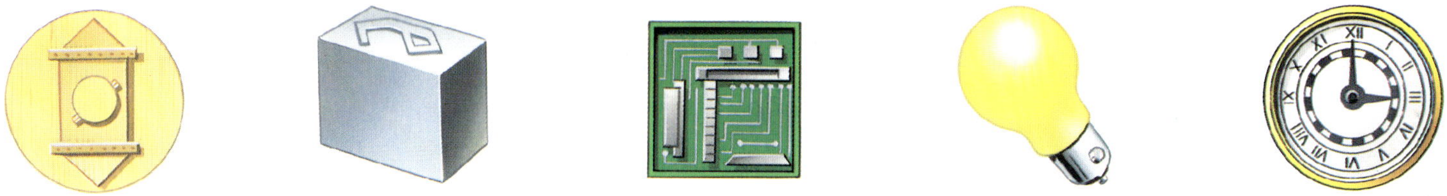

FLYING
MACHINES

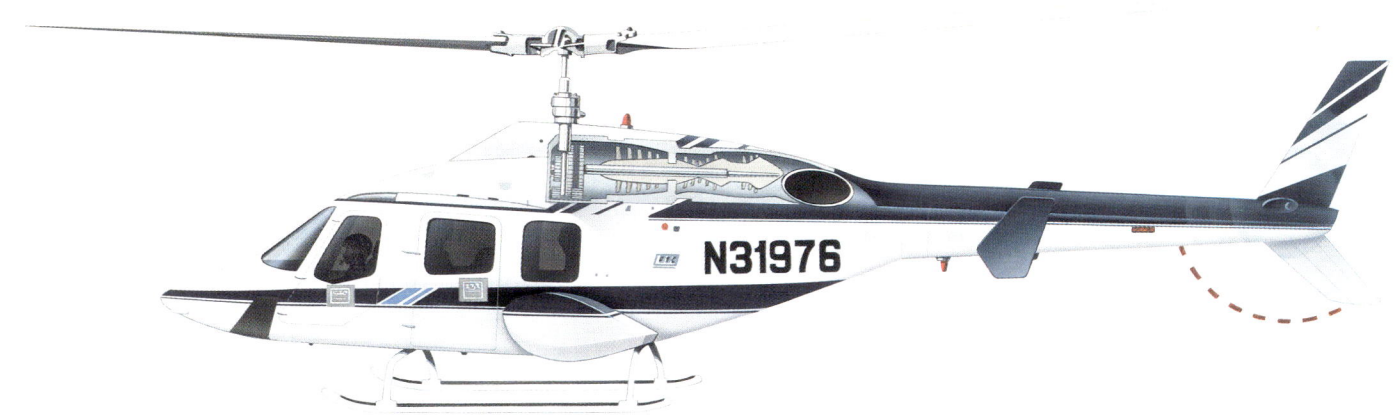

STEVE PARKER

GLOUCESTER PRESS
London • New York • Toronto • Sydney

© Aladdin Books Ltd 1993

All rights reserved

Designed and produced by
Aladdin Books Ltd
28 Percy Street
London W1P 9FF

First published in Great Britain in 1993 by
Watts Books
96 Leonard Street
London WC2A 4RH

A catalogue record for this book is available from the British Library.

ISBN: 0 7496 1343 2

Printed in Belgium

Design:	David West Children's Book Design
Designer:	Stephen Woosnam-Savage
Editor:	Jen Green
Picture researcher:	Emma Krikler
Illustrator:	David Russell

The author, Steve Parker, is a writer and editor in the life sciences, health and medicine, who has written many books for children on science and nature.

The consultant, Frazer Swift, works in the Interpretation Unit at the National Museum of Science and Industry, London.

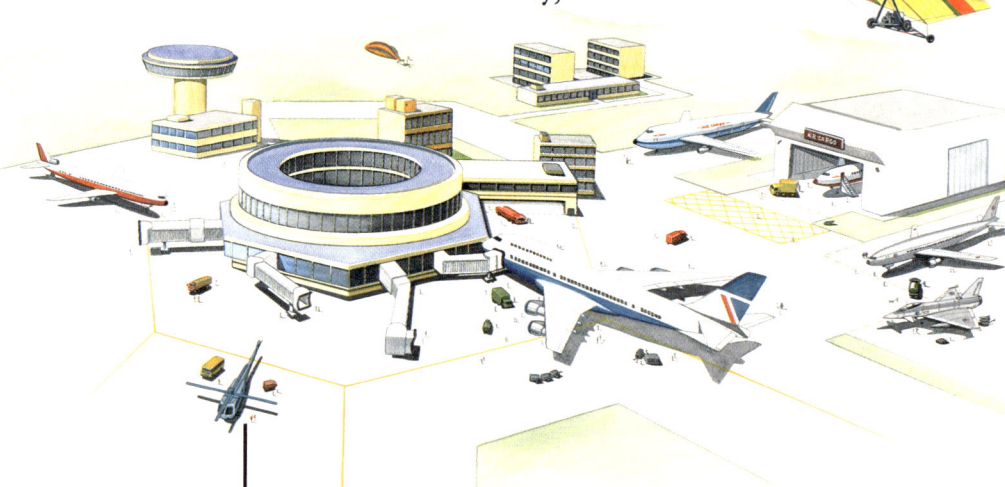

PHOTOCREDITS

Front cover top & pages 8, 9 *bottom*, 11 *bottom right*, 14 *top & bottom*, 15 *middle:* Roger Vlitos; *front cover bottom right*, 9 *top:* Mary Evans Picture Library; 5: Charles de Vere; 6 *both*, 10, 11 *bottom left*, 16, 26 *both:* Hulton Deutsch; 11 *top*, 15 *top & bottom*, 17 *top*, 20, 21 *top*, 22 *both*, 27, 28 *both:* Frank Spooner Pictures; 11 *middle*, 29 *top left & middle:* McDonnell Douglas; 14 *middle*, 25 *top & bottom:* Robert Harding Picture Library; 17 *bottom*, 21 *bottom:* Eye Ubiquitous; 18 *middle*, 24: British Aerospace; 18 *bottom*, 19: Airbus Industrie; 23 Spectrum Colour Library; 29 *top right:* Rolls Royce; 30 *top & middle*, 31 *bottom:* Valdagno Italia, Alitalia; 30 *bottom:* Boeing; 31 *top:* Hughes Helicopters

CONTENTS

THE INVENTION OF FLIGHT	4
PIONEERS OF FLIGHT	6
HOW PLANES FLY	8
THE AGE OF THE PROPELLER	10
THE JET AGE	12
THE CROWDED SKIES	14
FLYING TODAY	16
THE PLANE-MAKERS	18
MILITARY AVIATION	20
VERTICAL TAKE-OFF	22
SHORT TAKE-OFF	24
WORK AND PLAY	26
INTO THE FUTURE	28
CHRONOLOGY	30
GLOSSARY	31
INDEX	32

THE INVENTION OF FLIGHT

Flight has been one of the great technical challenges of the 20th century. The first powered flight was achieved less than a hundred years ago. Today we can fly to the other side of the world in less than a day. Aircraft are a common sight in the sky, from jetliners carrying holiday-makers and business travellers, to fighter planes in an air display, or helicopters on a rescue mission. This is the story of the invention of the flying machine, and of the developments in technology that have resulted in the aircraft of today. It is also the story of the benefits and problems that aircraft have brought to the modern world.

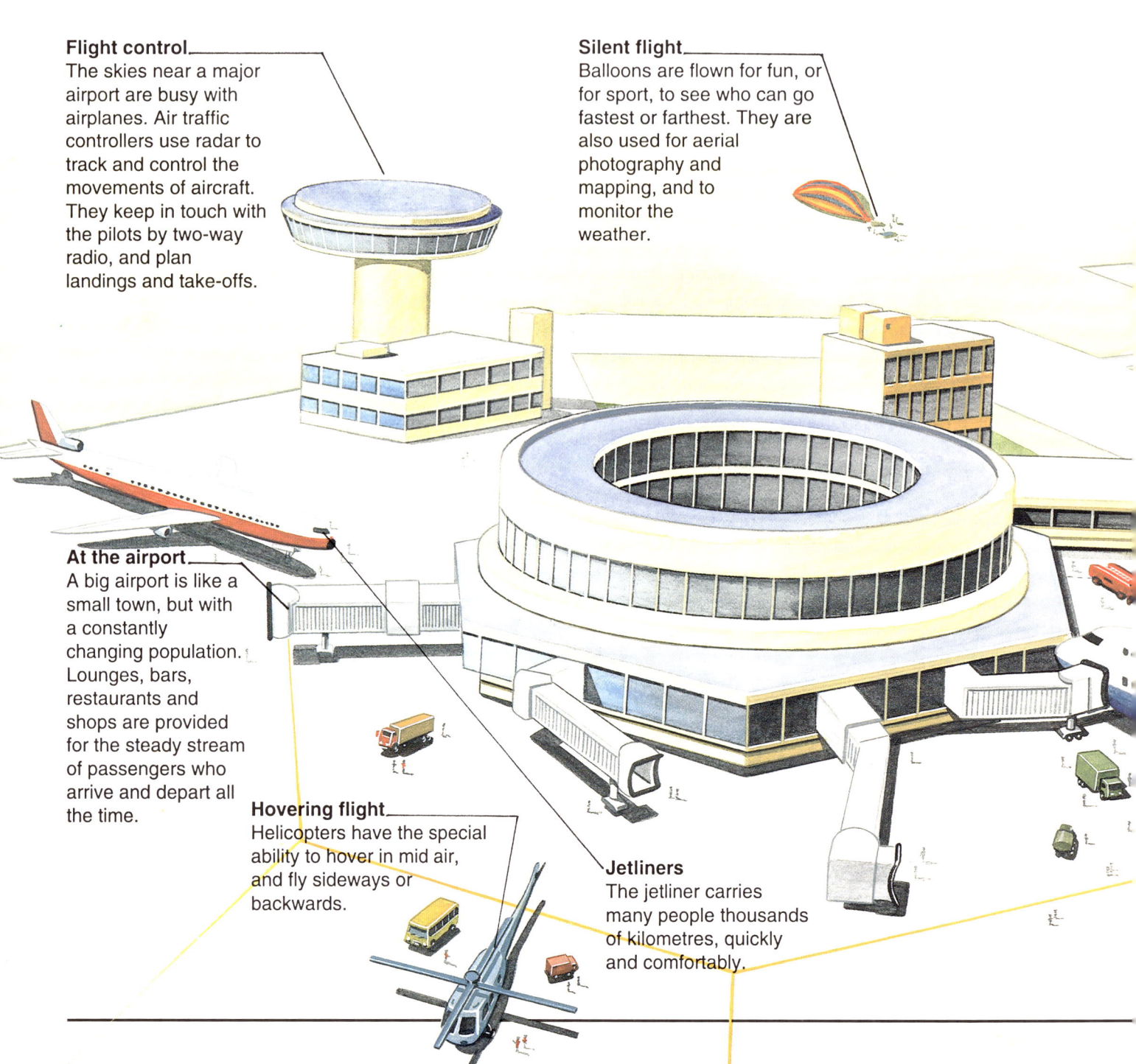

Flight control
The skies near a major airport are busy with airplanes. Air traffic controllers use radar to track and control the movements of aircraft. They keep in touch with the pilots by two-way radio, and plan landings and take-offs.

Silent flight
Balloons are flown for fun, or for sport, to see who can go fastest or farthest. They are also used for aerial photography and mapping, and to monitor the weather.

At the airport
A big airport is like a small town, but with a constantly changing population. Lounges, bars, restaurants and shops are provided for the steady stream of passengers who arrive and depart all the time.

Hovering flight
Helicopters have the special ability to hover in mid air, and fly sideways or backwards.

Jetliners
The jetliner carries many people thousands of kilometres, quickly and comfortably.

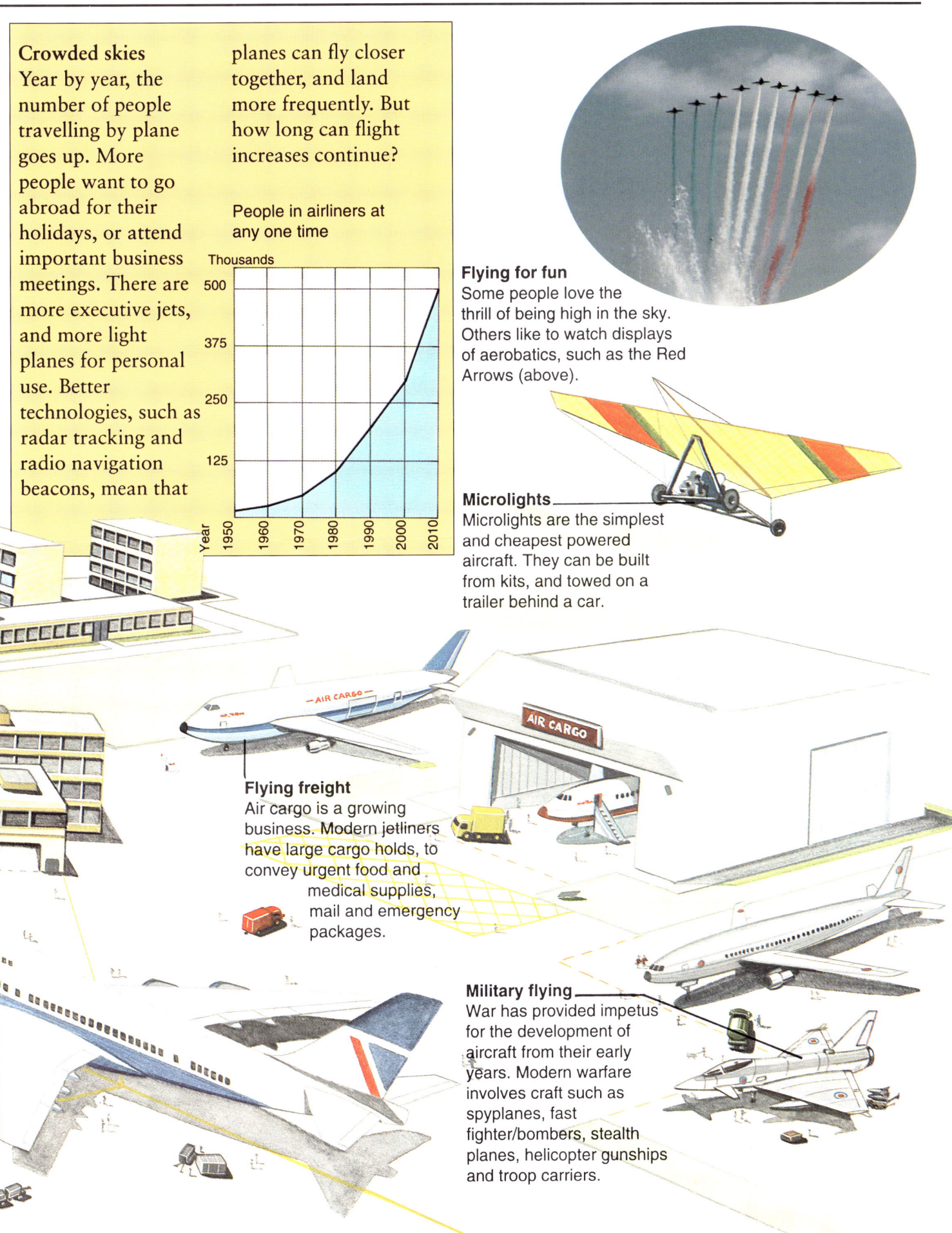

Crowded skies
Year by year, the number of people travelling by plane goes up. More people want to go abroad for their holidays, or attend important business meetings. There are more executive jets, and more light planes for personal use. Better technologies, such as radar tracking and radio navigation beacons, mean that planes can fly closer together, and land more frequently. But how long can flight increases continue?

People in airliners at any one time

Flying for fun
Some people love the thrill of being high in the sky. Others like to watch displays of aerobatics, such as the Red Arrows (above).

Microlights
Microlights are the simplest and cheapest powered aircraft. They can be built from kits, and towed on a trailer behind a car.

Flying freight
Air cargo is a growing business. Modern jetliners have large cargo holds, to convey urgent food and medical supplies, mail and emergency packages.

Military flying
War has provided impetus for the development of aircraft from their early years. Modern warfare involves craft such as spyplanes, fast fighter/bombers, stealth planes, helicopter gunships and troop carriers.

PIONEERS OF FLIGHT

In the early 1900s a number of inventors were trying to achieve powered flight. The Wright brothers made the first true airplane flight, in a heavier-than-air powered craft, in 1903. At first many believed that flying would have little effect on ordinary life. But when the first air show was held near Reims, in France, in 1909, 23 planes took part. Powered flight was here to stay.

Twin rudders for steering left and right

Muslin covering

Twin propellers turned by cogs and bicycle chains

Ash ribs in wing

Spruce bracing struts

First in the air
Balloons were the first flying machines, though they were not powered. The first balloon flight was made in November 1783, in France. The brothers Joseph and Jacques Montgolfier designed and built a hot-air balloon which flew almost 1,000 metres high. The Montgolfiers made many successful balloons.

Ideas for flight
Renaissance Italian artist and scientist Leonardo da Vinci thought about flight in the late 1400s. He designed various aircraft, some with flapping wings, which he called ornithopters. But they would have been too heavy to fly.

Gliding pioneer
A glider can be controlled in flight, and uses up-currents of air to go higher, but has no engine. The chief pioneer of gliding flight was the German engineer, Otto Lilienthal. He made hundreds of flights in gliders of his own design, in the 1890s. He crashed and died in 1896.

Orville Wright

Wilbur Wright

First in Britain

Samuel "Colonel" Cody, originally from Texas, was the first person to make a powered flight in Britain. His first flight was in a craft of his own design, in 1908. He also devised a method for using kites to lift military observers in baskets, to spy on the enemy (shown left).

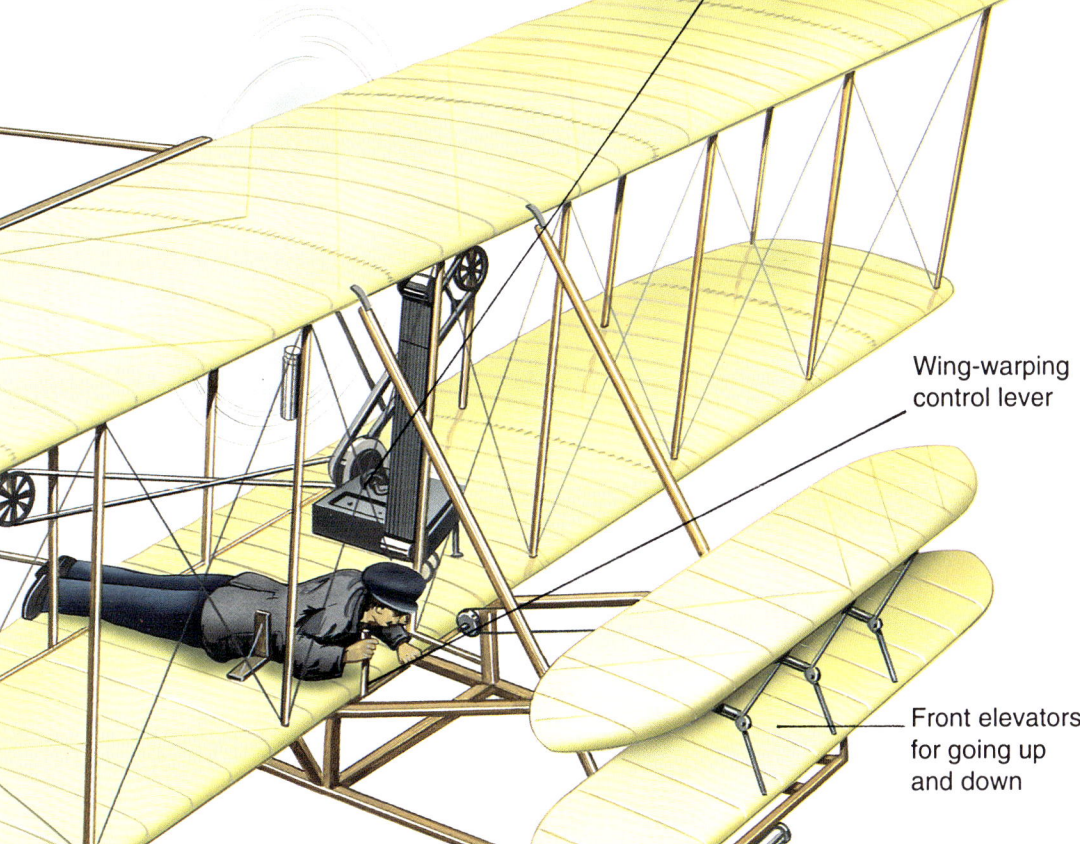

Engine
Wing-warping control lever
Front elevators for going up and down
Wright *Flyer*
Biplane (double-winged) design

Across The Channel

After the Wrights' pioneering efforts, the London *Daily Mail* newspaper offered a prize of £1,000 for the first plane flight across The Channel between England and France. The winner was Frenchman Louis Blériot. He made the crossing on 25 July 1909, in his tiny plane *Blériot No XI* (above).

Across the Atlantic

During World War I aircraft developed greatly. The challenge after the war was to fly across the Atlantic. John Alcock and Arthur Brown did this in June 1919, in a converted Vickers Vimy bomber.

First plane flight

The age of the plane began on a cold morning in December 1903, at Kitty Hawk in North Carolina. Orville Wright flew about 37 metres in 12 seconds, at 2-3 metres high, in the *Flyer*, designed and built with his brother Wilbur. The Wright brothers ran a bicycle business in Dayton, Ohio, which provided the money for their flying experiments. The key to their success was a lightweight, four-cylinder petrol engine. Although some early pioneers had experimented with steam-powered engines, only the internal combustion engine proved compact, yet powerful enough to propel a plane through the air.

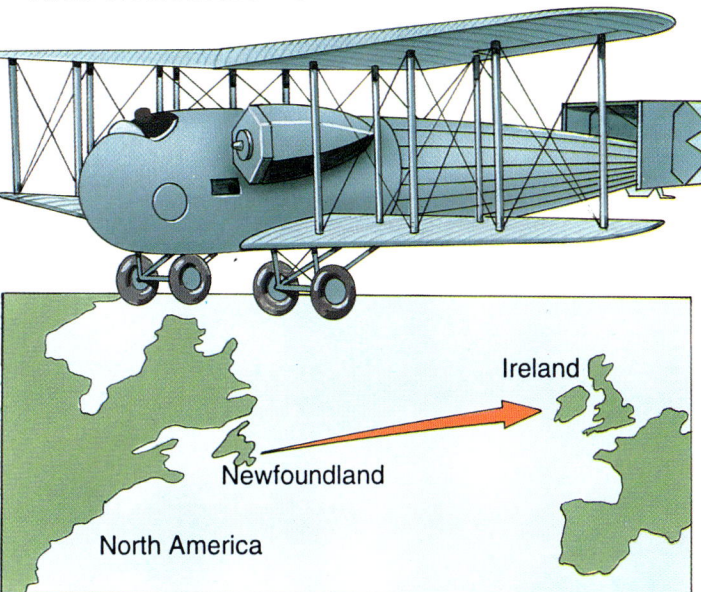

Route of Alcock and Brown

Ireland
Newfoundland
North America

How Planes Fly

Although the size, shape and engine layout of aircraft has changed over the years, most of today's planes have the same basic components. There is a central tube, the fuselage, to which the wings, tailplane and landing gear are attached. The fuselage of a jetliner is usually made of sections of metal. It may be pressurised to provide breathable air at high altitudes. Most aircraft have the basic design shown here.

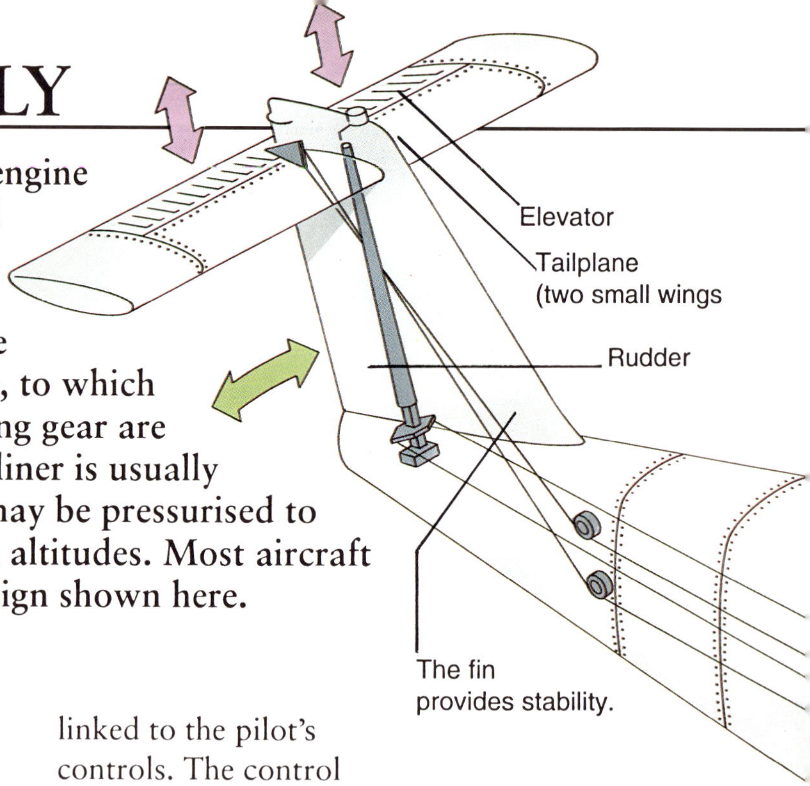

- Elevator
- Tailplane (two small wings
- Rudder
- The fin provides stability.

Staying in the air

The engine propels the plane forwards, but its wings keep it in the air. Seen from the side, the wing has a curved shape, the aerofoil section. Air flows faster over the more-curved upper surface. This creates lower air pressure above and higher air pressure below, and so the wing is "sucked" upwards by a force called lift. Moveable surfaces on the wings, the slats, flaps and spoilers, create more lift for take-off, or smoother streamlining for high-speed cruising.

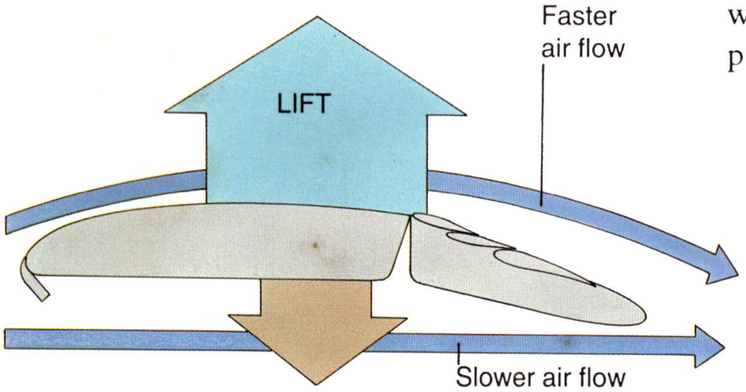

Control surfaces

A typical plane controls its direction through the air by three main types of control surfaces. These are the rudder (shown in green here), elevators (purple) and ailerons (orange). They are moved into the airstream rushing past, to twist or push the plane in a certain direction, as explained on the right. The control surfaces are moved by cables running around pulleys, which are linked to the pilot's controls. The control column (joystick) works the elevators and ailerons. The rudder pedals operate the rudder. In some larger aircraft the controls have hydraulic pumps or electric motors to assist movements.

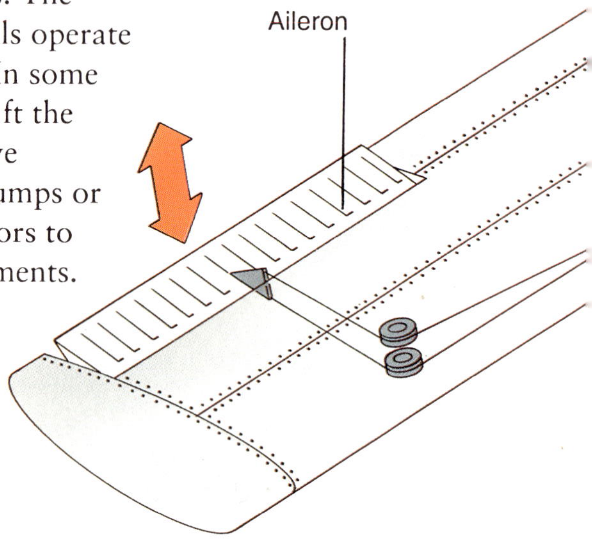

Aileron

LIFT
Faster air flow
Slower air flow

Wing-warping

Early airplanes such as the *Flyer* were controlled partly by wing-warping. Wires pulled on the ends of the flimsy, flexible wings and twisted them slightly out of shape, making the plane bank (turn).

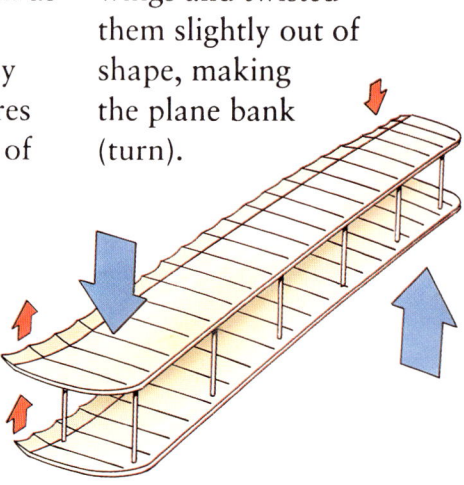

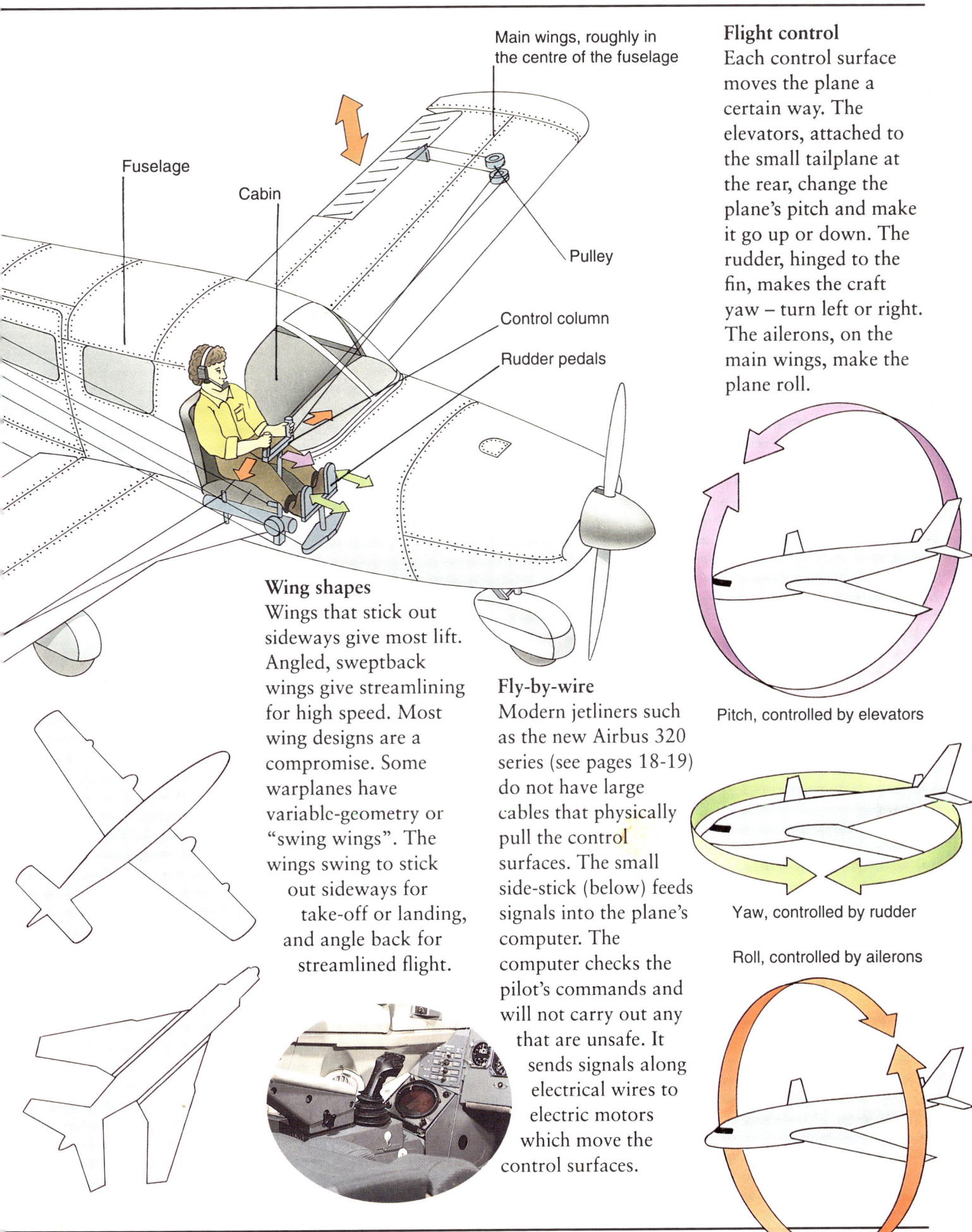

Flight control

Each control surface moves the plane a certain way. The elevators, attached to the small tailplane at the rear, change the plane's pitch and make it go up or down. The rudder, hinged to the fin, makes the craft yaw – turn left or right. The ailerons, on the main wings, make the plane roll.

Pitch, controlled by elevators

Yaw, controlled by rudder

Roll, controlled by ailerons

Wing shapes

Wings that stick out sideways give most lift. Angled, sweptback wings give streamlining for high speed. Most wing designs are a compromise. Some warplanes have variable-geometry or "swing wings". The wings swing to stick out sideways for take-off or landing, and angle back for streamlined flight.

Fly-by-wire

Modern jetliners such as the new Airbus 320 series (see pages 18-19) do not have large cables that physically pull the control surfaces. The small side-stick (below) feeds signals into the plane's computer. The computer checks the pilot's commands and will not carry out any that are unsafe. It sends signals along electrical wires to electric motors which move the control surfaces.

The Age Of The Propeller

Only a dozen years after the first powered flight, war planes were in action in World War I. They were used first for reconnaissance, and later as fighters and bombers. During the course of the war, airplanes developed from flimsy, open-air machines to highly manoeuvrable craft which provided good protection for the aviator. Their engines became powerful and reliable. After the war this technology was put to civilian use. The first airliners were built from bomber planes, but soon purpose-designed airliners were being made.

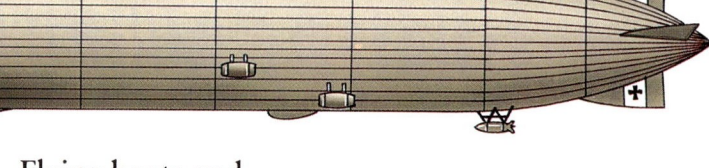

Graf Zeppelin

Propeller power

The first planes were moved by propellers. A "prop" spins around very fast and pushes air back, pulling the plane forwards. Early plane propellers were driven by lightweight piston engines, adapted from car or motorcycle engines. Soon engines were being specially designed for planes. The "rotary" engine was invented in 1909. Its cylinders were arranged in a circle around the central crankshaft. They rotated with the propeller while the crank stayed still. This solved the problem of keeping the engine cool, whilst the power generated was greatly increased.

Flying boats and airships

Flying boats like the Boeing 314 Clipper offered greater comfort to passengers. Even more luxurious were the vast airships of the Zeppelin company, but their life was short. A series of disasters culminated in the destruction of the *Hindenberg* in 1937, when 36 people died. This spelt the end of the airship era.

Interwar years

No sooner had the war ended than the first airlines were set up to carry fee-paying passengers. Britain's Imperial Airways launched their first service to Paris in 1924, and United Air Lines their flights between Chicago and San Francisco in 1934.

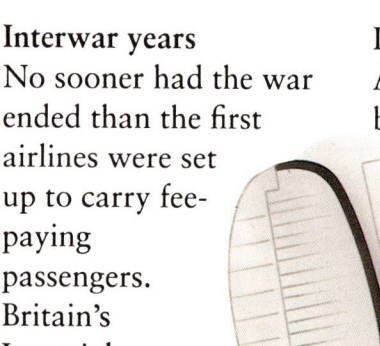

Boeing 314 Clipper

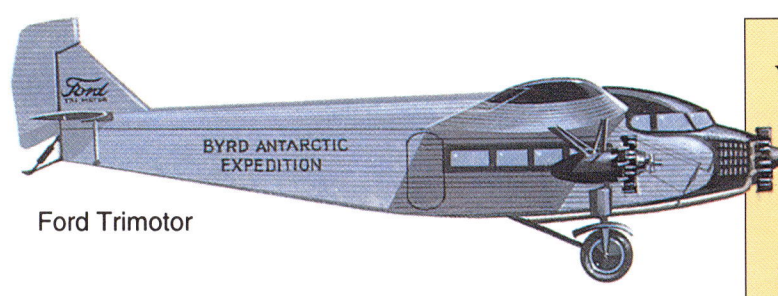
Ford Trimotor

The "Tin Goose"
The first passenger planes were noisy and cold. A new era of air transport was begun by the Ford Trimotor, one of the first planes built specifically to carry passengers. The "Tin Goose" had a passenger cabin constructed of thin metal plates fixed to a metal frame. It revolutionised aircraft design, and with its successors, the Boeing 247 and the Douglas DC-2, was the forerunner of today's airliners.

Women pioneers
Women, as well as men, made news with their trail-blazing flights. In 1930, Amy Johnson flew solo from England to Australia in 19 days. In 1932 Amelia Earhart became the first woman to fly solo over the Atlantic. She disappeared mysteriously on a round-the-world trip in 1937.

Douglas DC-3 Dakota

The boat-shaped hull of the flying boat allowed it to land and take off on a lake or sea. At the time there were few airports with long hard-surfaced runways.

From Supermarine to Spitfire
Advances made in air technology during the inter-war years were taken up by the military when World War II broke out. The technology behind the Supermarine seaplane, designed for speed-racing, was used in the development of the Spitfire fighter plane, so famous during World War II.

Postwar years
World War II saw an endless quest for ever-faster fighters, longer-range bombers, and increasingly sophisticated technology. The development of radar (see page 14) meant that aircraft could be "seen" at night. When the war ended, aircraft designed as warplanes were adapted for civilian use. The Douglas DC-3 Dakota, the most successful commercial airplane of all time, developed from the DC-1 and DC-2. Many are still in service around the world. The Boeing Stratocruiser was a direct descendant of the B29 bomber. It set new standards for trans-Atlantic flights.

Vickers-Supermarine Spitfire

THE JET AGE

In World War II, fast fighters such as the Spitfire, the Messerschmitt 109 and Mustang continued the development of warplane technology. But air forces wanted even greater speed to outfly the enemy, and there is a limit to the speed at which propeller-driven aircraft can fly. The result was the jet engine. Although jet fighters took part in combat, they arrived too late to have a great effect on the war's outcome. But by the 1950s, jet-powered planes were in service.

The first jets

Jet engines were developed in the 1930s, in England by Frank Whittle and his team, and in Germany by Hans von Ohain and his co-workers. The first jet plane to fly was a German test version, the Heinkel He 178, in August 1939. The Gloster Whittle was another early jet plane, powered by one of Whittle's engines. The first jet plane to enter military service was the RAF's Gloster Meteor, in July 1944.

The developing jet

In the years following World War II, aero engineers searched for new metals and alloys (combinations of metals) that could withstand the enormous temperatures inside the jet engine, and the heat caused by great friction when flying through the air at such tremendous speed.

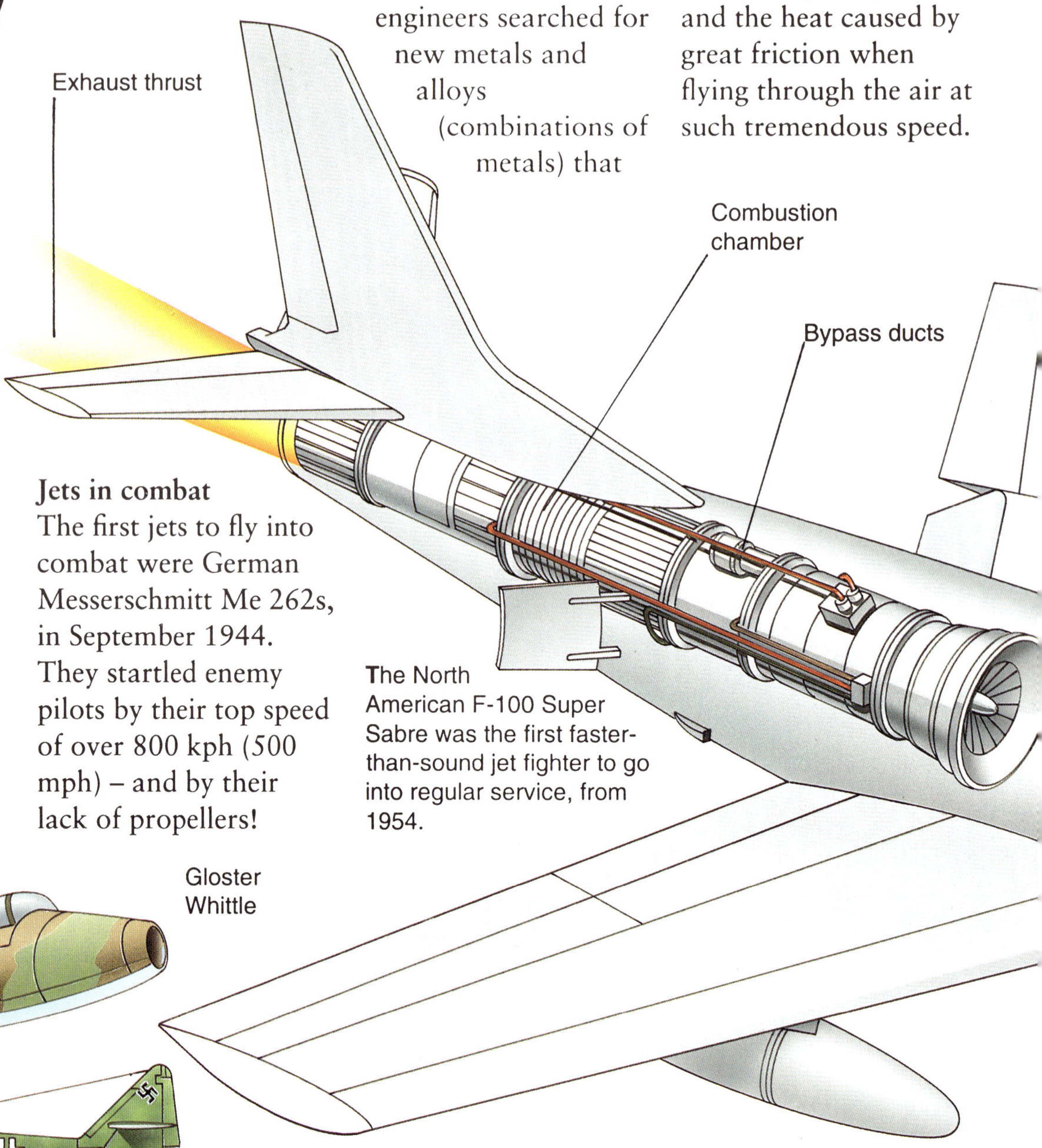

Jets in combat

The first jets to fly into combat were German Messerschmitt Me 262s, in September 1944. They startled enemy pilots by their top speed of over 800 kph (500 mph) – and by their lack of propellers!

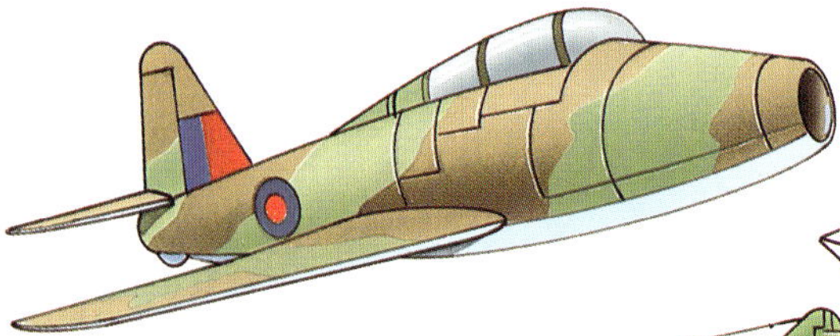

Exhaust thrust

Combustion chamber

Bypass ducts

The North American F-100 Super Sabre was the first faster-than-sound jet fighter to go into regular service, from 1954.

Gloster Whittle

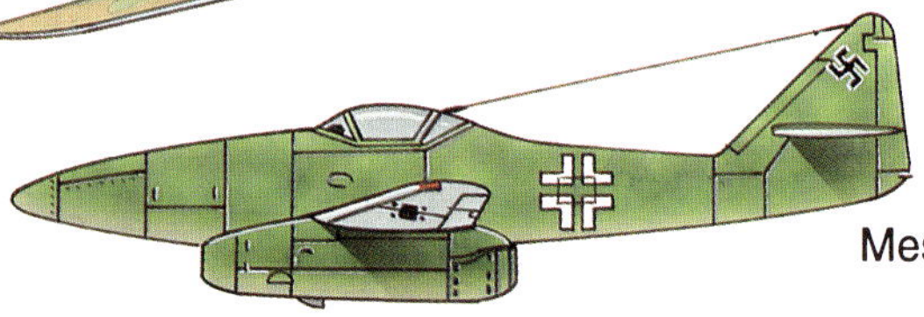

Messerschmitt Me 262

How the jet works

A gas turbine or turbojet draws in air, compresses (squashes) it, mixes it with fuel, and sets fire to it in a type of continuous explosion. The heated air expands, and forces its way out of the exhaust pipe, creating the "jet" of hot gases that gives the engine its nickname.

There are several types of jet design. Most modern jetliners are powered by turbofan engines, shown below. The engine gets its name from the huge fan-shaped turbine at the front. This blows air around the main engine, and also sucks air inside the engine, where a set of smaller turbines spin round rapidly to compress it. The compressor is driven by another set of turbines in the exhaust system, which is turned by the hot gases blasting out of the back.

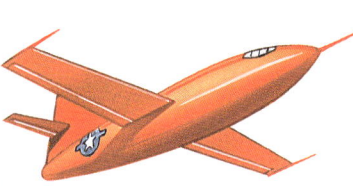

The sound barrier

Today's jets regularly fly faster than sound. In the 1940s, many people thought that flying faster than sound was impossible. As planes approached that speed, they were buffeted by powerful shockwaves. Charles "Chuck" Yeager first broke the sound barrier safely on 14 October 1947, in the Bell X-1 rocket plane, above.

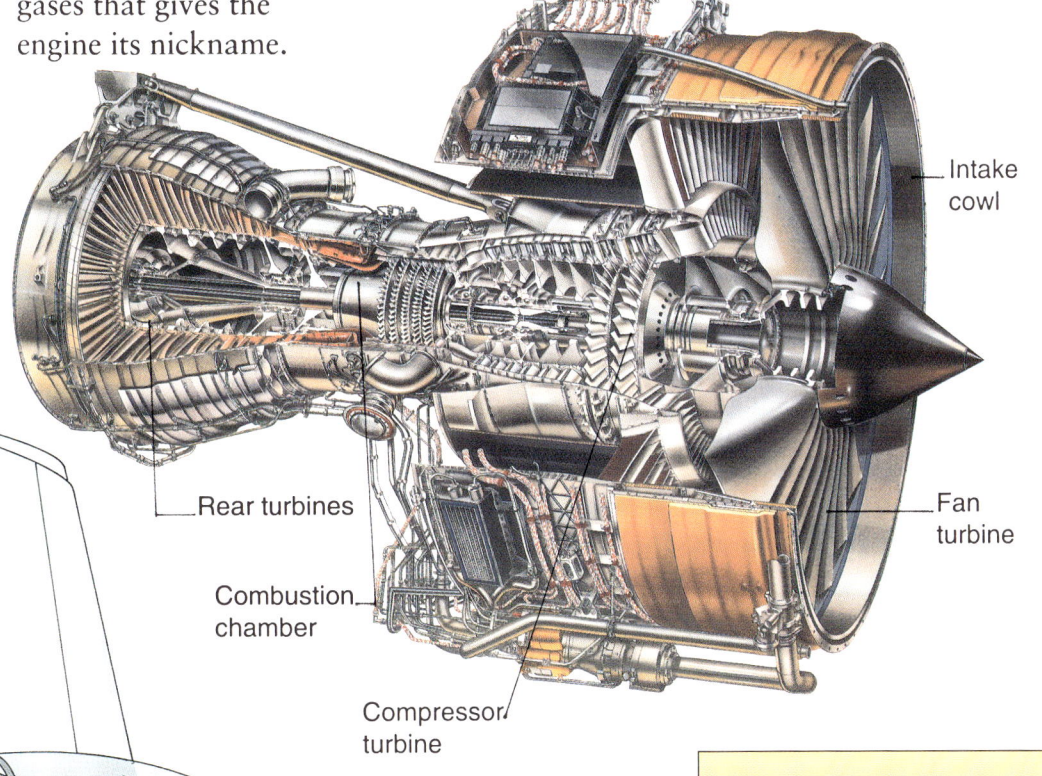

- Intake cowl
- Rear turbines
- Fan turbine
- Combustion chamber
- Compressor turbine
- Jet air intake
- Nose intake

Jet airliners

The first jet-powered passenger plane was the British de Havilland Comet, below, test-flown in 1949, and in regular service by 1952. It was eventually overtaken in numbers of planes by the US Boeing 707.

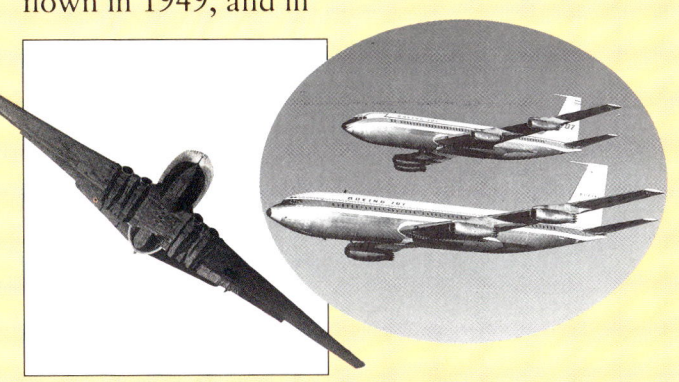

THE CROWDED SKIES

The first pilots carried a few maps, an accurate timepiece and a magnetic compass to help them navigate. Our skies are now hundreds of times busier, with planes flying ten times faster. Air Traffic Control (ATC) has become increasingly sophisticated. Before each flight the crew are given a detailed flight plan. ATC gives permission for take-off, and clears the plane's flight through international airlanes to its destination.

Borrowed from boats Pioneer aviators navigated with the help of star charts and the sextant, left. This measures the angle between the horizon and the Sun, Moon, star or planet.

A great invention Radar means RAdio Detection And Ranging. Like many inventions, radar was developed in war time, in this case, during World War II. A radar transmitter sends out radio signals, and the receiver picks up echoes which bounce back from any objects in range. Each "blip" on a radar screen represents an aircraft. The picture shows British radar operators in the 1960s.

1 Weather radar
2 ILS Localiser receiver
3 ILS Glidescope receiver
4 VHF communications aerial
5 Satellite communications aerial
6 Radio altimeters
7 Omega aerial
8 VOR receiver
9 Avionics bay

On-board navigation
Once airborne, it is vital for pilots to know exactly where they are. Planes possess many navigation systems, above, and the technology of navigation improves almost monthly. Radio signals are transmitted by special ground-based radio beacons, or by aircraft themselves, to aid navigation. Plane radar receivers can show the bearing, or direction, that the radio signals come from. The aircraft's transponders transmit a positive identification signal and a height reading.

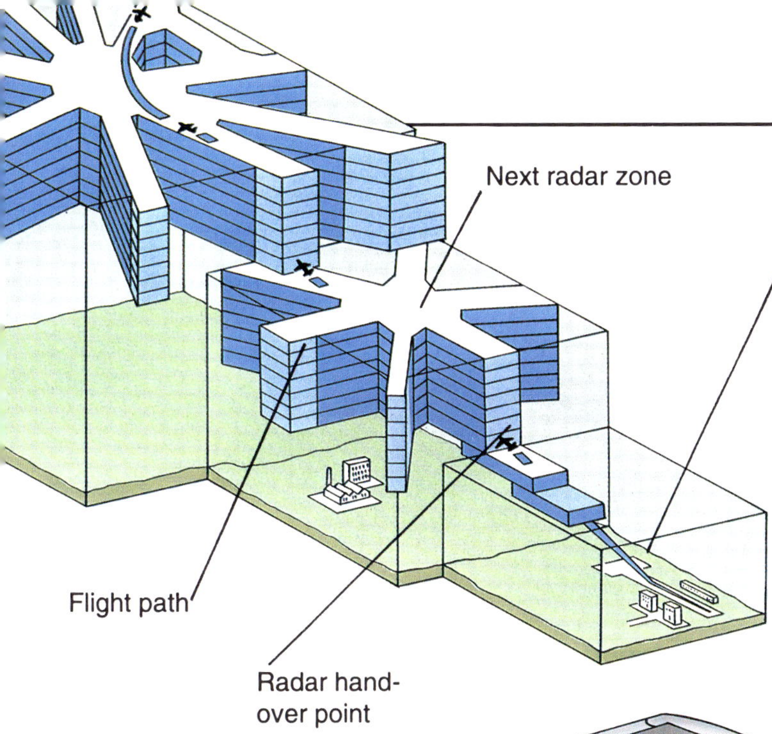

Next radar zone

Airport control zone

Cleared for take-off
On take-off (shown left), an aircraft follows a closely defined path through crowded airspace whilst it climbs to its planned cruising height. It cannot proceed from the air zone controlled by Air Traffic Control at the airport until it has gained enough height. At a radar hand-over point responsibility for the aircraft passes to the next sector.

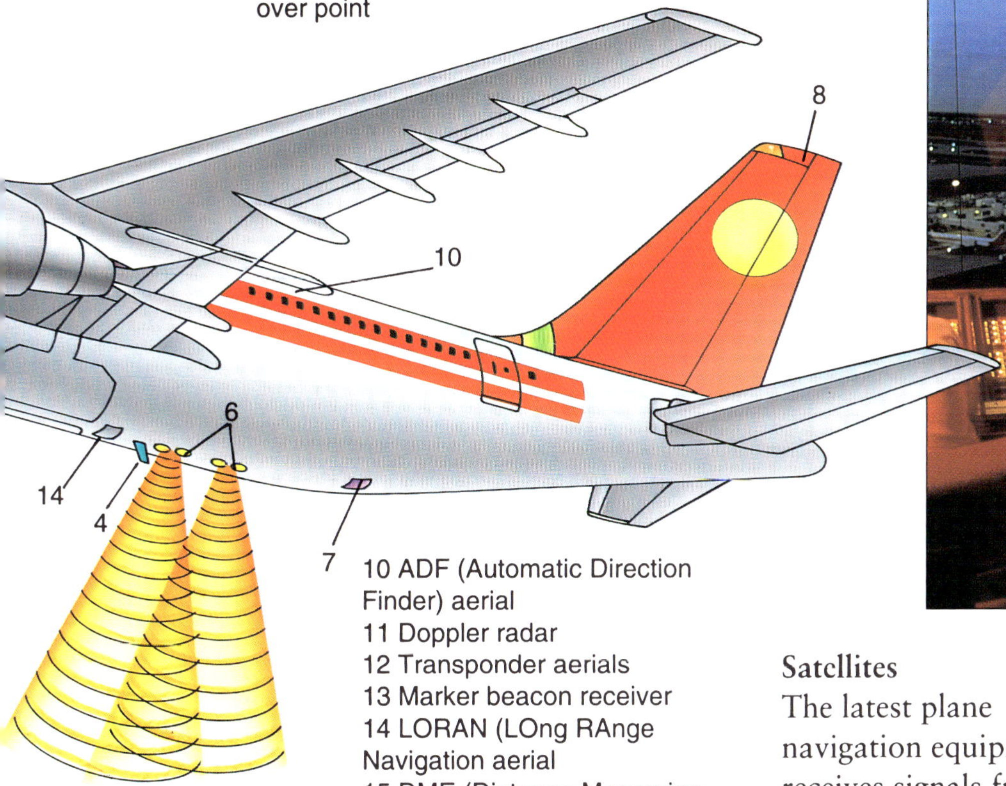

Flight path

Radar hand-over point

10 ADF (Automatic Direction Finder) aerial
11 Doppler radar
12 Transponder aerials
13 Marker beacon receiver
14 LORAN (LOng RAnge Navigation aerial
15 DME (Distance Measuring Equipment) aerials

Flight paths
The skies round a major airport are divided into pathways and corridors, marked by VOR (Very high-frequency Omni-directional Range) beacons. While a plane waits to land it queues, or "stacks", circling round and round at a certain height over a beacon in the vicinity. When instructed by ATC, it proceeds to the next-lowest level, and ultimately to a stack near the airport itself. Finally, it is given the all-clear for final approach and landing.

Satellites
The latest plane navigation equipment receives signals from below, and also above, from satellites orbiting the Earth. The NAVSTAR navigation system provides signals from at least four satellites at any one time. The in-flight navigation computer calculates the craft's position at any one instant to the nearest 100 metres.

The Air Traffic Control centre monitors all aircraft in the vicinity by radar and radio, and clears them for landing and take-off.

15

FLYING TODAY

Running a modern airline is a multi-billion-pound business. It employs many thousands of people, from plane designers and engineers to the ground crew who service and maintain planes, and from check-in and security staff at the airport, cooks and cleaners behind the scenes, to the crew of the aircraft itself. Provided the demand is sufficient, the faster a plane can be refuelled and "turned around", the more money it makes. But many airlines today face severe financial difficulties. In 1992 alone airlines around the world lost 5.3 billion dollars.

Check-in
For most flights, passengers must book in advance. They arrive an hour or two before take-off, to claim their seats, and go through security and passport checks.

Airline comfort
Today's passenger cabins are easy to service and are roomy enough for passengers to move about in – an important factor since some flights now last more than 20 hours non-stop.

Bigger and faster
In the 1960s, fast, reliable long-distance aircraft such as the Boeing 707 and the Douglas DC-8 made flying more popular. The Boeing 747 Jumbo Jet, which entered service in the early 1970s, continued the trend. At 70 metres long and with a wingspan of 59 metres, it is still the world's largest airliner. The double-decker Big Top versions carry over 500 people. Fastest is still the BAC-Aerospatiale Concorde, cruising at 2,150 kph (1,350 mph), with 130 passengers. Both planes were developed during the 1960s.

Airline wars
Like any business, an airline must make money. The battle for passengers is fierce. Pan American Airlines (Pan-Am) began in 1927, and operated Boeing 707s in the 1950s. But it disappeared in the world recession of the late 1980s and early 1990s. Most countries have a "national" airline. Their advertising appeals to the patriotic feelings of their citizens.

Concorde

Boeing 747

On the ground

A plane must be refuelled, serviced (left) and inspected by engineers – all in about 30 minutes. Up-to-date airliners bristle with safety features and safety regulations. The speed and efficiency of emergency services at airports are tested regularly (right).

Cabin staff have been employed on airliners since in 1930s. They serve meals and drinks, and attend to passengers' requests and problems.

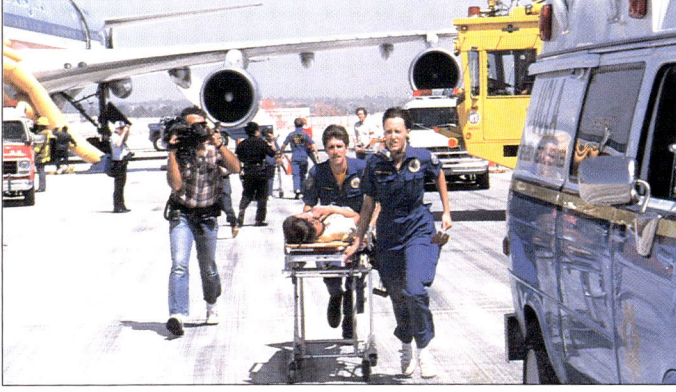

More space

Since the 1960s, plane-makers have tried to fit more people into each airliner, to make it more efficient in terms of fuel and costs. The standard fuselage size, as on the short-distance Douglas DC-9, has been widened on some of the Airbus series, because its jet engines can carry extra weight. The Big Top Boeing 747 has an extended upper cabin behind the flight deck.

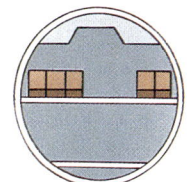

Normal fuselage
Douglas DC-9

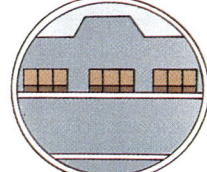

Wide body
Airbus 340

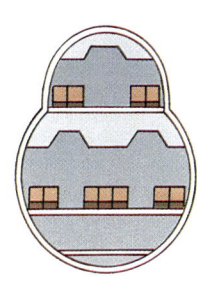

Big Top
Boeing 747-300

Security

Planes have become the target for many terrorist threats, both from individuals and from organised terrorist groups. Because of this, security at airports becomes stricter every year. Passengers are questioned about the contents of their luggage, as shown above, and they may be searched. Baggage passes through an X-ray scanner, and suspicious items are investigated.

An easy target

Terrorism has increased in recent years. The bomb that caused the mid-air explosion of a Pan-Am airliner over Lockerbie, Scotland, in 1988, shocked the world (below). It brought questions about whether planes should transport baggage that does not belong to someone on board. It also raised the issue of whether terrorist warnings, received by airlines almost daily, should all be acted upon, even though most are false alarms.

The Plane-Makers

Plane-building is big business. The manufacturers Boeing and McDonnell Douglas in the United States and Airbus Industrie in Europe are giant companies. There are arguments as to how much each of these companies is funded either directly or indirectly by its government. At the factory work proceeds simultaneously on past, present and future models. Some workers service planes built many years ago, whilst others research the aircraft of the future.

Better by design

The invention of computer-aided design (CAD) revolutionised aircraft production. A new plane can have its fuselage widened by a few centimetres or be fitted with a new seating layout in a few minutes on screen. Market research on safety and comfort is taken into account, and fuel-economy tests run. Computer programmes are not foolproof, and wind-tunnel tests of real scaled-down models show up unforeseen problems.

Jobs in the industry

In the long term, air travel is continuing to expand, although there have been fat and lean years for the industry. Plane-builders have suffered from world recessions and the fear of terrorism. Computers, automation and robot workers have meant the loss of many jobs. With the ending of the Cold War, military programmes have also faced cutbacks. The EFA Eurofighter currently being developed by teams from Britain, Spain and Germany was nearly cancelled, but was reinstated because about 100,000 jobs were at stake.

The fuselage is made in sections that fit together for rivetting and welding.

The fuel pipes, electrical and hydraulic systems in the wings are connected to the flight deck controls.

Built for strength

Jetliners today have a stressed-skin or single-body construction, pioneered on the Monocoque Deperdussin of 1912. The skin of the central fuselage is built to withstand great pressure, and is strengthened with ribs and hoops to prevent it from bending or collapsing. The fuselage of this European Airbus is joined to the wings, cockpit and tail sections in the factory in Toulouse, France.

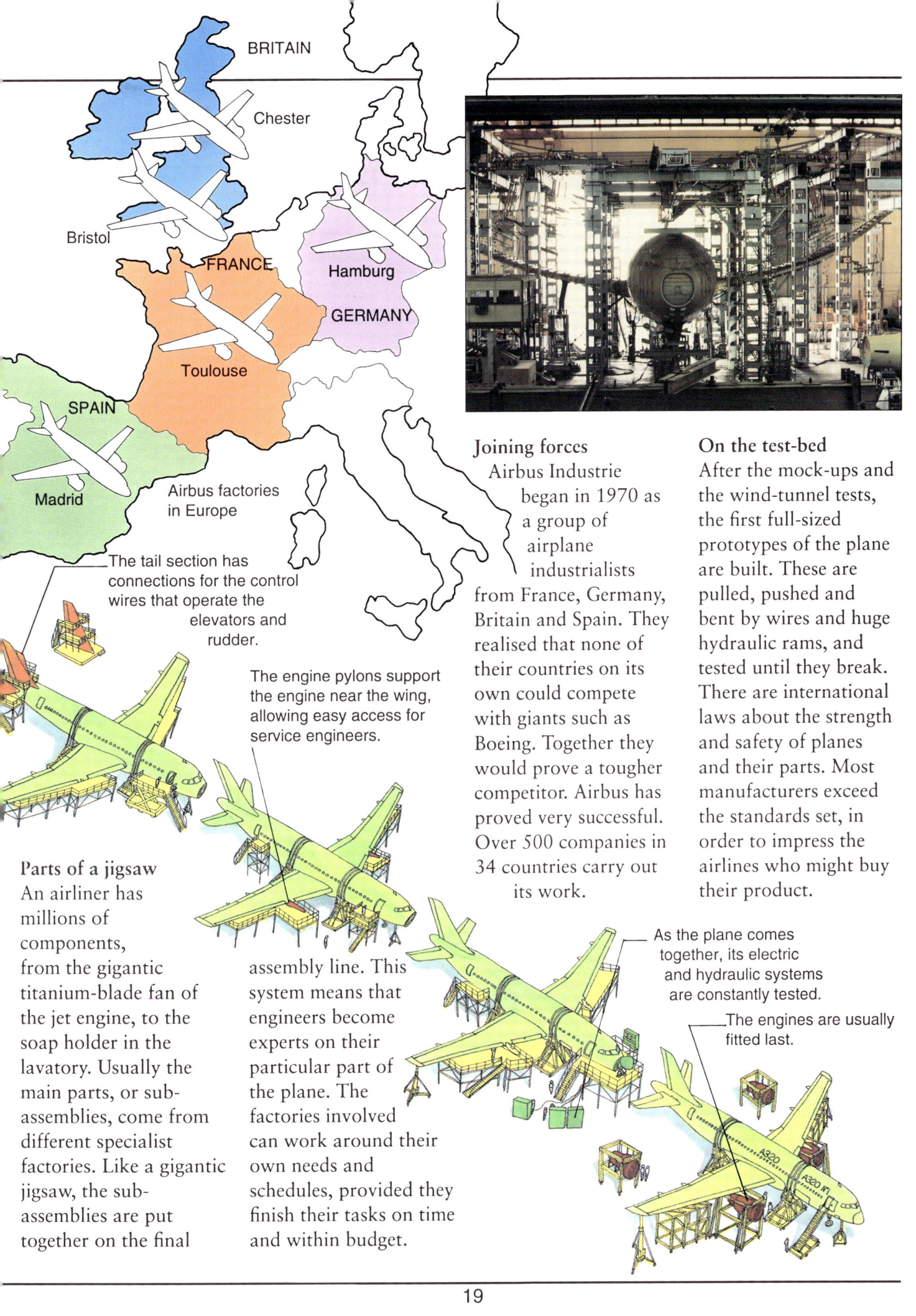

Airbus factories in Europe

The tail section has connections for the control wires that operate the elevators and rudder.

The engine pylons support the engine near the wing, allowing easy access for service engineers.

As the plane comes together, its electric and hydraulic systems are constantly tested.

The engines are usually fitted last.

Parts of a jigsaw

An airliner has millions of components, from the gigantic titanium-blade fan of the jet engine, to the soap holder in the lavatory. Usually the main parts, or sub-assemblies, come from different specialist factories. Like a gigantic jigsaw, the sub-assemblies are put together on the final assembly line. This system means that engineers become experts on their particular part of the plane. The factories involved can work around their own needs and schedules, provided they finish their tasks on time and within budget.

Joining forces

Airbus Industrie began in 1970 as a group of airplane industrialists from France, Germany, Britain and Spain. They realised that none of their countries on its own could compete with giants such as Boeing. Together they would prove a tougher competitor. Airbus has proved very successful. Over 500 companies in 34 countries carry out its work.

On the test-bed

After the mock-ups and the wind-tunnel tests, the first full-sized prototypes of the plane are built. These are pulled, pushed and bent by wires and huge hydraulic rams, and tested until they break. There are international laws about the strength and safety of planes and their parts. Most manufacturers exceed the standards set, in order to impress the airlines who might buy their product.

Military Aviation

In less than a century warplanes have developed beyond recognition. The first dogfight between two aircraft took place in October 1914. Since then, air power has been decisive in almost every major war. Today's warplanes carry a wide variety of armaments, including fast-firing cannons, and sophisticated guided missiles and bombs. Some planes, such as the Stealth fighter and the F-15 Eagle, are developed for one purpose only. "Multi-role" warplanes are designed to be able to carry out different functions by modifying a basic aircraft frame.

Fokker Dr-1 Triplane, maximum speed 165 kph (103 mph)

World War I pilot dressed in warm clothes against the cold

Early warplanes

World War I planes were manoeuvrable but had few technological aids. The pilot relied on his own flying skills. The top flying ace was German pilot Manfred von Richthofen, known as the "Red Baron", above. His planes – an Albatros, and later a Fokker Triplane – were painted scarlet. Official war records show that he shot down 80 enemy planes, before being killed in 1918.

World War II

Different planes had different roles during World War II. Fighters were small and fast, but could not carry many armaments or fly long distances. Bombers such as the Boeing B-29 Superfortress shown here were bigger, with enough fuel for long flights. But they were slower, and vulnerable to enemy fighters.

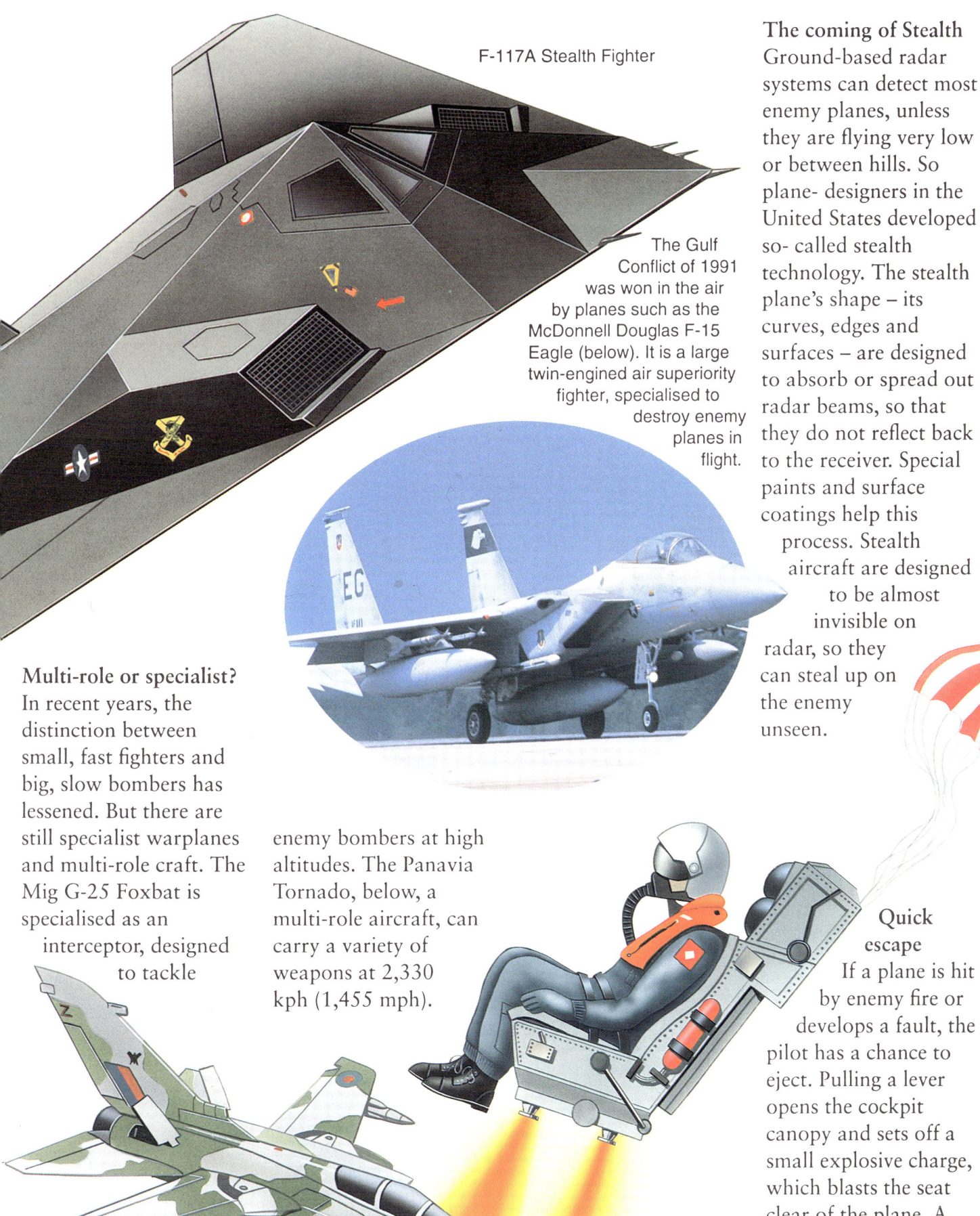

F-117A Stealth Fighter

The Gulf Conflict of 1991 was won in the air by planes such as the McDonnell Douglas F-15 Eagle (below). It is a large twin-engined air superiority fighter, specialised to destroy enemy planes in flight.

The coming of Stealth
Ground-based radar systems can detect most enemy planes, unless they are flying very low or between hills. So plane-designers in the United States developed so-called stealth technology. The stealth plane's shape – its curves, edges and surfaces – are designed to absorb or spread out radar beams, so that they do not reflect back to the receiver. Special paints and surface coatings help this process. Stealth aircraft are designed to be almost invisible on radar, so they can steal up on the enemy unseen.

Multi-role or specialist?
In recent years, the distinction between small, fast fighters and big, slow bombers has lessened. But there are still specialist warplanes and multi-role craft. The Mig G-25 Foxbat is specialised as an interceptor, designed to tackle enemy bombers at high altitudes. The Panavia Tornado, below, a multi-role aircraft, can carry a variety of weapons at 2,330 kph (1,455 mph).

Quick escape
If a plane is hit by enemy fire or develops a fault, the pilot has a chance to eject. Pulling a lever opens the cockpit canopy and sets off a small explosive charge, which blasts the seat clear of the plane. A parachute opens, and the pilot sinks to safety.

VERTICAL TAKE-OFF

The modern helicopter took shape in the 1930s. Early attempts at VTOL – Vertical Take-Off and Landing – lifted off the ground, but were unstable. In 1939 Russian-born Igor Sikorsky came up with the experimental VS-300. This pioneering design established the basic layout and control system of the helicopter which has been followed ever since. In the 1950s the invention of the turboshaft engine led to the rapid development of helicopters for many purposes. Today they are used as attack aircraft, transport vehicles, rescue craft and even for intercity commuting.

Sikorsky's VS-300 prototype (1939)

Rotary wings
The helicopter flies because its wings move fast through the air, rather than the air moving fast over the wings.

Lift is provided by rotors – rotating wings with the typical curved aerofoil shape of a normal plane wing.

The rotors
A rotor blade has an aerofoil section. As it whirls around, it creates low air pressure above, and gets sucked upwards by the force of lift, like an ordinary wing (see page 8). The helicopter's body does not have to move forward for lift to be created. The amount of lift is controlled by the speed of the rotors through the air, and the angle of tilt of their blades, known as the pitch. The pilot adjusts the pitch of the rotors to make the helicopter move forwards or backwards.

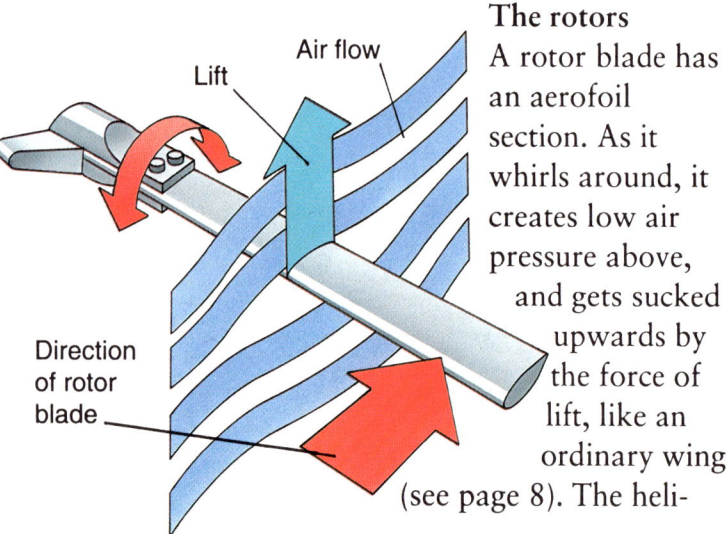

Heavy-lift helicopters can transport large loads.

The Boeing Vertol-Chinook

Best of both worlds?
The Bell-Boeing V-22 Osprey has an unusual design. The engine-and-propeller units at the end of its wings swivel from the horizontal to the vertical. The aircraft uses its rotors to take off vertically like a helicopter, then the units swivel so that the machine flies forward like a normal airplane. This design poses many mechanical difficulties, although prototypes have flown successfully.

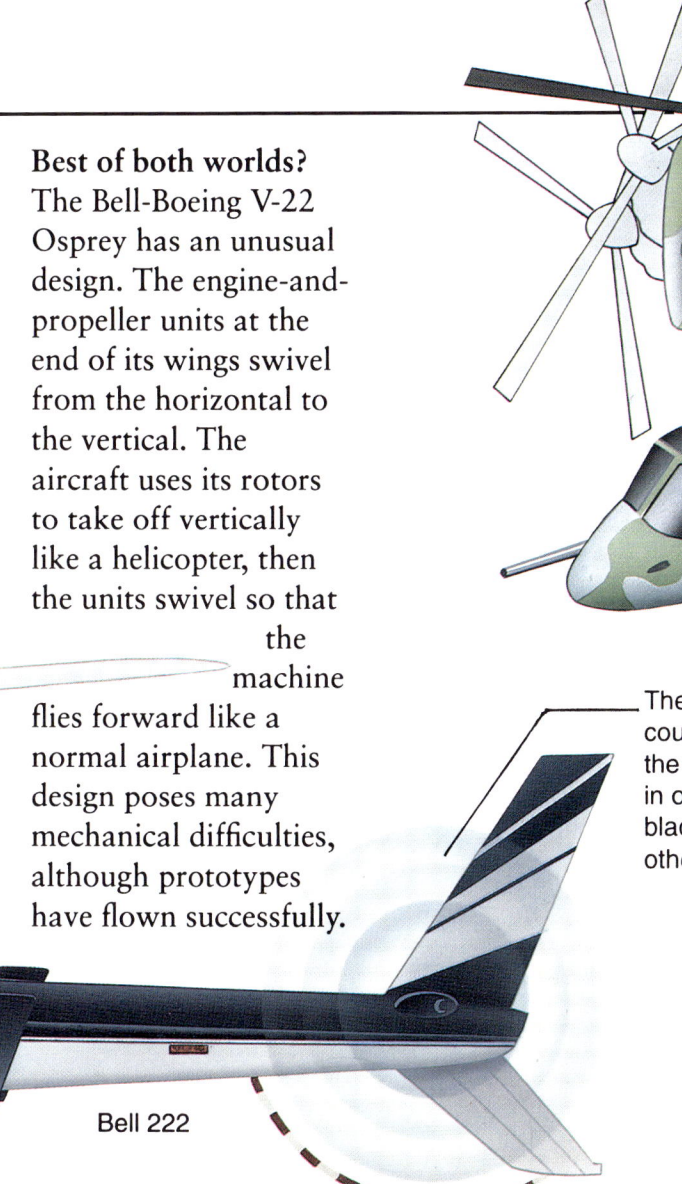

Bell-Boeing V-22 Osprey

The small tail rotor counteracts the tendency of the helicopter body to rotate in one direction as the main blades spin very fast the other way.

Bell 222

VTOL jets
The British Harrier "Jump Jet" is an ingenious invention. The thrust of its Pegasus jet engine is directed through four nozzles, two in each side of the fuselage. These can be swivelled to point down for vertical take-off and hovering, and then backwards for normal flight. This makes the Harrier manoeuvrable and adaptable, and ideal for aircraft carrier use. This very successful design is being built for the US Marines.

Search and rescue
The manoevrability of helicopters make them ideal for traffic-spotting, crowd surveys, landing in city centres or other small areas, and SAR (Search And Rescue). They can hover over any type of terrain, from a steep cliff to the open ocean, and winch people by cable to safety.

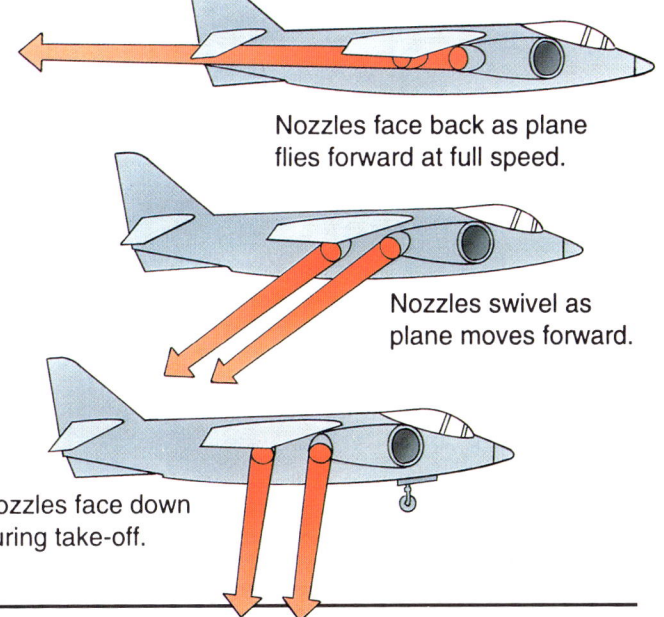

Nozzles face back as plane flies forward at full speed.

Nozzles swivel as plane moves forward.

Nozzles face down during take-off.

SHORT TAKE-OFF

Helicopters are versatile flying machines, but are costly to service and maintain. Their fuel consumption is high, especially on longer flights. An alternative is the Short Take-Off and Landing (STOL) plane. STOL craft are designed to use an airstrip of only a few hundred metres. Civilian craft operate from short runways near city centres. Military STOL planes can land on rough airstrips close to front-line troops. On an aircraft carrier, STOL aircraft are launched and landed with the help of a catapult from a runway of just a few dozen metres.

The autogyro
The autogyro was invented by Spanish engineer Juan de la Cierva in 1923. This tiny flying machine has a small engine that powers a pusher-propeller. The large rotor is not moved by the engine, but turns around by itself. This gives the autogyro a short take-off run, less than 50 metres in some cases.

The auto-rotor
The autogyro's large overhead rotor is pushed around by the flow of air past it, as the craft moves forwards. This produces lift, which pulls the autogyro skywards like a helicopter.

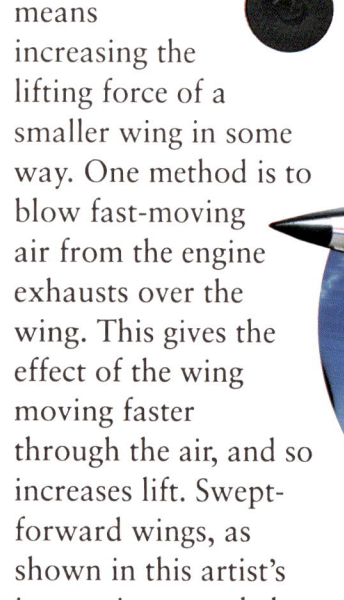

Military STOL
Planes that can fly from short, rough airstrips have long interested the armed forces. Technically, there are two ways to produce an aircraft that can take off in a very short distance. One is to increase the area of the wings, to give more lift. But long, wide wings cause problems at high speed. The other is called lift augmentation, which means increasing the lifting force of a smaller wing in some way. One method is to blow fast-moving air from the engine exhausts over the wing. This gives the effect of the wing moving faster through the air, and so increases lift. Swept-forward wings, as shown in this artist's impression, may help.

24

Steep climber
The de Havilland Canada Dash-7 is one of the most successful of the large STOL passenger planes. It has a design typical of STOL aircraft, with wings set high on the fuselage, and a high T-tail. The Dash-7 is powered by four extremely quiet turboprop engines. It carries up to 54 people. The plane can take off in 690 metres (2,260 feet), becoming airborne so quickly, and climbing so steeply, that many passengers say it is like going up in an elevator!

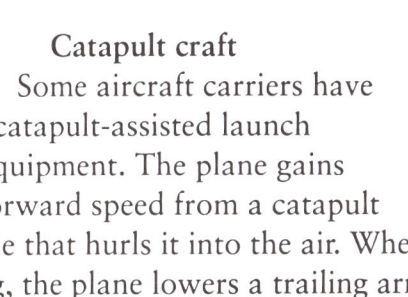

Catapult craft
Some aircraft carriers have catapult-assisted launch equipment. The plane gains forward speed from a catapult cable that hurls it into the air. When landing, the plane lowers a trailing arm with a small hook. This catches a cable laid across the runway deck, and drags it along. Hydraulic machinery slows the cable, bringing the plane to a halt.

The BAe 146, shown above, is a small four-engined jet that combines excellent STOL capabilities with a low level of engine noise.

◀ An artist's impression of a military STOL plane with swept-forward wings is shown opposite.

Flying into the city
Most large planes need long runways, and create noise that disturbs people nearby. So airports are usually on the city outskirts. It is time-consuming for business travellers to reach these airports. Some cities now have airports almost in the centre, such as London's Docklands Airport. STOL aircraft use the short runway, and climb rapidly so their noise soon fades.

WORK AND PLAY

The past 20 years have seen an enormous growth in private flying. There are now many ways to fly for fun, but all amateur pilots must pass examinations before they are let loose in the skies. Generally the cheapest aircraft are the smallest. Tiniest of all powered craft are microlights, which are like motorised hangliders and can pack onto a car. Working planes perform many different tasks, in addition to carrying passengers and freight.

Ailerons

Hang-gliders
The modern hang-glider has a lightweight frame of metal tubes and cables, and a flexible wing of air-proof, tear-proof material. The pilot controls the glider by shifting his or her body weight.

Lightweight construction

One-person planes
Amateur fliers do not necessarily need to spend large amounts of money on their sport, since many craft are owned by clubs, and can be hired by the hour or day. Piloting a plane by yourself, alone in the sky, can be an exhilarating experience. Training takes place in a two-seater version, where the instructor demonstrates the basic controls and how to navigate.

Gliders
A glider has long, thin wings for sustained, soaring flights. It has no engine, so must be winched into the air on a long cable or towed up by a powered craft. A glider always sinks in relation to the air around it. But it can gain height in relation to the ground by spiralling in rising currents of air known as thermals.

Clear cockpit cover

Gaining height
Air moves upwards as it blows against a slope. Or it may rise where it is warmed by bare rock. The pilot circles in this updraught, and so gains height.

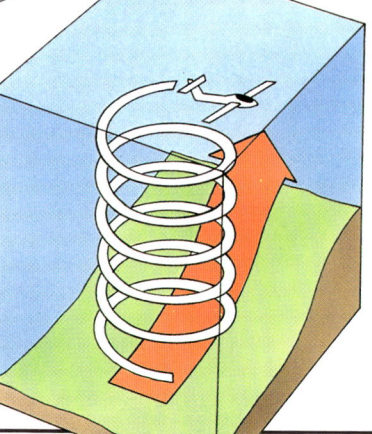

26

Kit planes

It is possible to build a plane in a space the size of a living room! Plane kits are less expensive than ready-made planes, because money is saved on assembly. The purchaser builds and assembles the plane, which can be enjoyable in itself. But such craft must be thoroughly checked and certified before they can be flown.

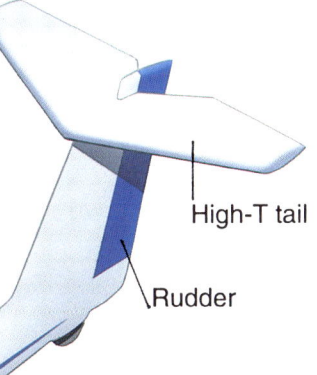
High-T tail
Rudder

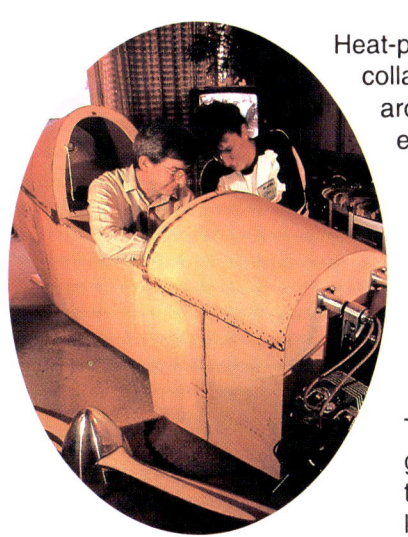

Ballooning

The balloon consists of a passenger basket and an envelope of tough fabric, which is filled with hot air. Warm air is lighter than cool air, and so rises, lifting the balloon. The heat comes from a flame roaring from a burner, fuelled by propane gas in metal bottles.

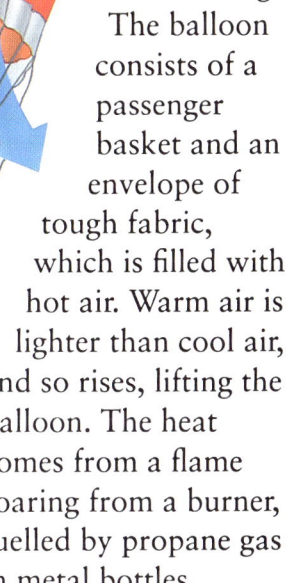
Heat-proof collar around envelope
Burner
The wickerwork gondola absorbs the shock of landing

Bizjets

Travelling by scheduled flights takes time. Some companies have their own executive planes. These small aircraft carry about 10-14 passengers at cruising speeds of 800 kph (500 mph). Travellers may use the telephone, fax and computer on board.

Working planes

The Canadair CL-215 is an adaptable transport plane, available in many versions. One is specialised for fire-fighting (shown right). It can skim over a lake or sea and scoop up over 5,000 litres (1,100 gallons) of water, then dump this onto a fire. Small planes fitted with spraying or dusting bars can quickly spread pesticides (below).

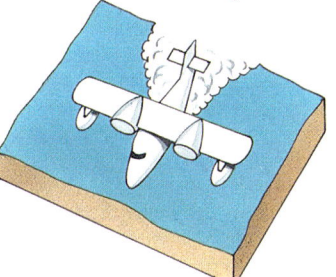

INTO THE FUTURE

What is the future of flight? Vast amounts of money and resources are used in the design and construction of each new plane. Military users have pioneered many advances in aircraft technology, but with the ending of the Cold War, military projects face cutbacks. Flying is a fast way to travel, but is inefficient in terms of fuel consumption compared to road, rail or ship. Aircraft pollute the high atmosphere with their exhaust gases, and the skies around airports with their noise and smell. But millions of people are employed in the air industry, and millions more rely on the privilege of air travel for business and holidays.

Bigger planes?
Some flight experts predict that planes will get even bigger. It is more economical to carry lots of passengers in one huge plane than in several small planes. This works well for long-haul (long distance) routes. There is also a future for smaller, quieter, and economical commuter aircraft that hop between city centres. Passenger planes are becoming ever more specialised for different jobs.

Artist's impression of Boeing 747 super double-decker

Too big
The Hughes H4 Hercules flying boat was designed and built by American billionaire Howard Hughes. Its wingspan was 97.5 metres (320 feet). Called the "Spruce Goose" because of its sprucewood construction, it flew only once, in 1947, with Hughes at the controls. It was simply too large, and its engines too weak.

Busier skies?
People who live near major airports suffer noise, smell and extra traffic. Airlines want easier travel for their customers, but local residents want a peaceful, less polluted life. These requirements bring the two sides into conflict. These protesters in Japan are campaigning against a new airport, which they feel could blight their lives.

Bigger airports?

As more people travel by air, so airports have to cope with them. If planes accommodate more passengers in the future, there may be even longer queues at ticket checks, passport controls and baggage reclaim. Airport designers face problems similar to those in huge sports stadiums, where thousands of people come and go in a rush, then the building is left almost empty. And there are always the considerations of safety and security.

Possible designs for super-jumbo jets of the future

Bigger engines?

More powerful jet engines are being designed to lift bigger planes into the air. The turbofan is the favoured design. The original Rolls Royce Trent was the first turboprop engine to fly. The name has been revived for the latest family of giant turbofans.

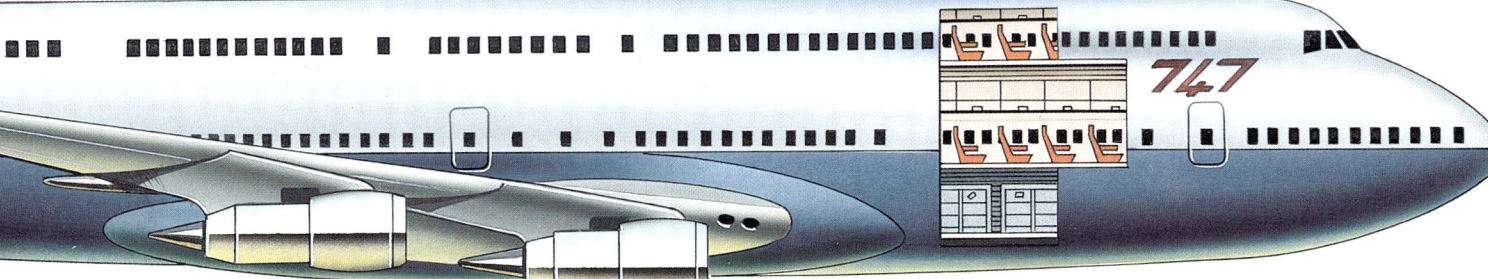

Double-decker

A proposal for the Boeing 747 Jumbo Jet is to make the whole fuselage double-decked, to accommodate over 800 passengers. But more powerful engines would be needed to carry the extra weight.

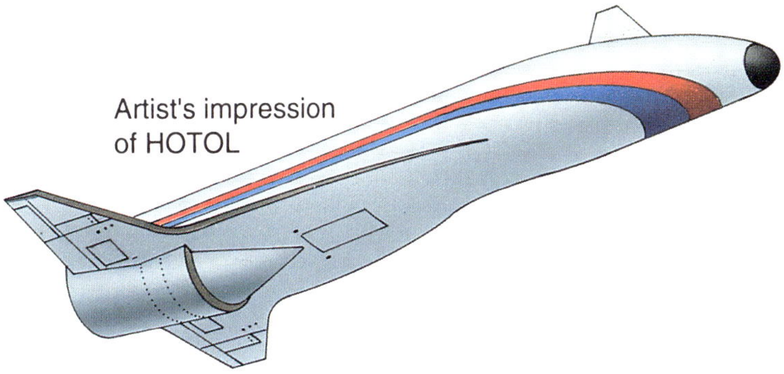

Space-planes

Plane-makers are exploring the possibility of craft that could fly in space, but take off and land using a normal runway. One proposal, the British HOTOL (HOrizontal Take-Off and Landing), has special engines that work conventionally in Earth's atmosphere and as rockets in space. The project may prove too costly, with not enough demand. Surveys show that most people are content to fly at normal speed and altitude, and take a few hours extra, rather than see billions of pounds spent on a project with limited benefits to the very few.

Artist's impression of HOTOL

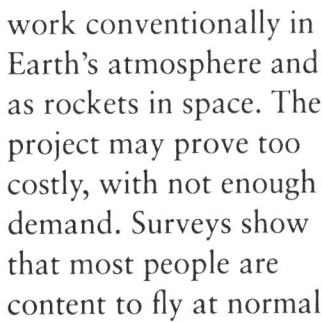

CHRONOLOGY

1783 First manned ascents, in Montgolfier hot-air balloons
1849 George Cayley experiments with gliders
1852 First airship flight by Henry Giffard, Paris
1874 Frenchman Félix du Temple's steam-powered craft almost becomes airborne
1890 Frenchman Clément Ader's steam-powered *Eole* almost flies
1891-96 Otto Lilienthal makes many successful gliding flights
1900 First Zeppelin airship flies in Germany
1903 First flight in a true airplane by Wright Brothers
1906 First plane flight in Europe, by millionaire Alberto Santos-Dumont in *14-bis*
1907 French inventor Paul Cornu experiments with early helicopters
1909 First plane flight across the Channel, by Louis Blériot
1909 First air show, near Reims in France
1910 First regular air passenger service by airship, between Germany and Sweden
1914 First regular air passenger service, between the US cities of St Petersburg and Tampa, Florida
1919 First non-stop plane flight across the Atlantic, by Alcock and Brown
1920s Air mail services begin
1927 First solo trans-Atlantic flight, by Charles Lindberg
1930 Amy Johnson is the first woman to fly solo from England to Australia
1930 Boeing Air Transport introduce air stewardesses
1930s "Golden Age" of airships and flying boats
1931 Britain's Supermarine S6B wins Schneider seaplane trophy
1932 Amelia Earhart is first woman to fly the Atlantic solo non-stop
1935 First flight of the Douglas DC-3 Dakota
1937 *Hindenberg* disaster ends the airship era
1937 Test-bench firings of Frank Whittle's Unit No 1, first jet engine
1939 Igor Sikorsky designs and flies the VS-300 helicopter,
1939 First flight by a jet plane, the Heinkel He178, in Germany
1940 Boeing Stratoliner is first airliner with pressurised cabin
1947 Charles Yeager is first to fly supersonic in Bell X-1 rocket plane
1949 US Air Force B-29 Superfortresses drop atomic bombs on Japan, ending World War II
1949 Maiden flight of first passenger jetliner, de Havilland Comet
1951 Bell X-5 is first swing-wing plane
1954 Maiden flight of Boeing 707 jetliner
1967 Bell X-15 rocket plane becomes the fastest winged craft, at 7,274 kph (4,520 mph)
1969 Maiden flights of first supersonic jetliner,

▲ Graf Zeppelin

Charles Lindberg's plane, *Spirit of St Louis*

▼ Boeing Stratocruiser

GLOSSARY

▲ Apache helicopter

Concorde, and Boeing 747 Jumbo
1972 First flight of Airbus A300 prototype
1973 First flight of an electric plane, MB-E1
1976 Lockheed SR-71A Blackbird sets speed record for a conventional jet plane, at 3,529

▲ Airbus A 300

kph (2,193 mph)
1977 Two jumbo jets collide in Tenerife, killing 583 people
1986 Dick Rutan and Jeanna Yeager are first to fly round the world non-stop, in *Voyager*
1987 Boeing 737 becomes world's best-selling jetliner

1987 Airbus A320 uses "fly by wire"
1988 Terrorist bomb destroys Pan Am Boeing 747 flight over Lockerbie, Scotland
1989 First flight of Northrop B-2 Stealth Bomber

1992 *October* Israeli Boeing 747 crashes, killing 70. *December* Dutch DC-10 crashes, killing 54. *December* Libyan Boeing 727 crashes, killing 158.
1993 Boeing 747 Cargo engine locking pins redesigned after crashes

Aerofoil section
The shape of an aircraft's wing when seen from the side, with a greater curvature on the upper surface, to produce a lifting force.

Ailerons
Moveable control surfaces, usually on the outer rear edges of the main wings, that make the plane roll (bank or tilt) to the left or to the right.

CAD
Computer-Aided Design, using computers to help design items such as cars and aircraft.

Elevators
Moveable control surfaces, usually on the tailplane (small rear wings), that make the plane go up or down.

Fuselage
The main body of a plane, usually shaped like a long tube.

Pitch
One of the three directions of movement of an aircraft. It means to point up or down, so as to ascend or descend.

Radar
RAdio Detection And Ranging, a system that detects the reflected echoes of radio waves, for navigation and detecting objects.

Roll
One of the three directions of movement of an aircraft. It means to tilt or bank to one side or the other, following a corkscrew-like path.

Rotary-winged craft
An aircraft in which the wings whirl round and round, such as a helicopter or autogyro.

Rudder
Moveable control surface, usually on the rear of the fin (upright "tail"), that makes the plane turn left or right.

Sound barrier
The speed of sound, which must be exceeded to fly supersonic. At sea level it is reached at about 1,226 kph (761 mph).

Stealth
Technology in which a plane's shape and surface coverings are designed to minimise radio reflections and so make it less noticeable to radar.

Turbofan
A type of jet engine with a very large-bladed turbine or "fan" at the front.

Yaw
One of the three directions of movement of an aircraft. It means to swing to the left or right, like a car being turned left or right.

INDEX

aerobatics 5
aerofoil section 8, 22, 31
ailerons 8, 9, 31
air cargo 5
air shows 6
Air Traffic Control (ATC) 4, 14, 15
Airbus Industrie 9, 17, 18-19
airliners 10, 11, 16, 17, 19, 28, 29
airlines 10, 16-17, 28
airports 4, 11, 15, 25, 28, 29
airships 10
Alcock, John and Brown, Arthur 7
autogyro 24

balloons 4, 6, 27
Bell-Boeing V-22 23
Blériot, Louis 7
Boeing 747 Jumbo Jet 16, 17, 29
Boeing Stratocruiser 11
bomber planes 5, 10, 11, 20, 21

cabin staff 17
catapult-assisted launch equipment 24, 25
check-in 16
Cody, Samuel 7
computer, in-flight 9, 15
computer-aided design (CAD) 18, 31
Concorde 16
control column (joystick) 8
control surfaces 8, 9
crop-spraying planes 27

de Havilland Canada Dash- 7, 25
de Havilland Comet 13

design 8-9, 18
Douglas DC-3 Dakota 11

Earhart, Amelia 11
ejecting 21
elevators 8, 9, 31
executive planes 27

fighter planes 4, 5, 11, 12, 18, 20, 21
fire-fighting planes 27
flaps 8
flight paths 15
flying boats 10, 11, 28
Ford Trimotor ("Tin Goose") 11
fuselage 8, 17, 18, 29, 31
future of flight 28-9

gliders 6, 26

hang-gliders 26
Harrier Jump Jet 23
helicopters 4, 5, 22-3, 24
Hindenberg 10
history of flight 30-1
HOrizontal Take-Off and Landing (HOTOL) planes 29
Hughes H4 Hercules ("Spruce Goose") 28

internal combustion engine 7

jet engine 12-13, 29
jetliners 4, 5, 8, 9, 13, 18
Johnson, Amy 11

kit planes 27
kites 7

landing 15

Leonardo da Vinci 6
lift 8, 22, 24
lift augmentation 24
Lilienthal, Otto 6

McDonnell Douglas F-15 Eagle 20, 21
Messerschmitt Me 262 12
microlights 5, 26
military planes 5, 9, 10, 11, 12, 18, 20-1, 24, 28
Montgolfier brothers 6
multi-role planes 20, 21

navigation 14, 15

passenger cabins 11, 16
pioneers 6-7
piston engine 10
pitch 9, 22, 31
plane manufacture 17, 18-19, 29
pollution 28
powered flight, first 6-7
private flying 26-7
propellers 10
prototypes 19

radar 4, 5, 11, 14-15, 21, 31
radio navigation beacons 5, 14
Red Arrows 5
Richthofen, Manfred von ("Red Baron") 20
roll 9, 31
rotary engine 10
rotary-winged craft 22, 23, 24, 31
rudder 8, 9, 31

safety 17, 19
satellites 15
Search and Rescue (SAR) 23
security 17
sextant 14
Short Take-Off and Landing (STOL) planes 24-5
single-body construction 18
slats 8
sound barrier 12, 13, 31
space-planes 29
spoilers 8
spyplanes 5
stacking 15
stealth planes 5, 20, 21, 31
Supermarine Spitfire 11, 12
swing-wing planes 9

take-off 14, 15
terrorism 17, 18
tests and inspections 17, 18, 19
thermals 26
transport planes 27
troop carriers 5
turbofan engine 13, 29, 31

Vertical Take-Off and Landing (VTOL) craft 22-3

Whittle, Frank 12
wing-warping 8
wings 8, 9, 24
women aviators 11
World War I planes 10, 20
World War II planes 11, 12, 20
Wright brothers 6, 7

yaw 9, 31
Yeager, Charles 13